Animals &ME

Elephants and Me

Sarah Harvey

Explore other books at:
WWW.ENGAGEBOOKS.COM

VANCOUVER, B.C.

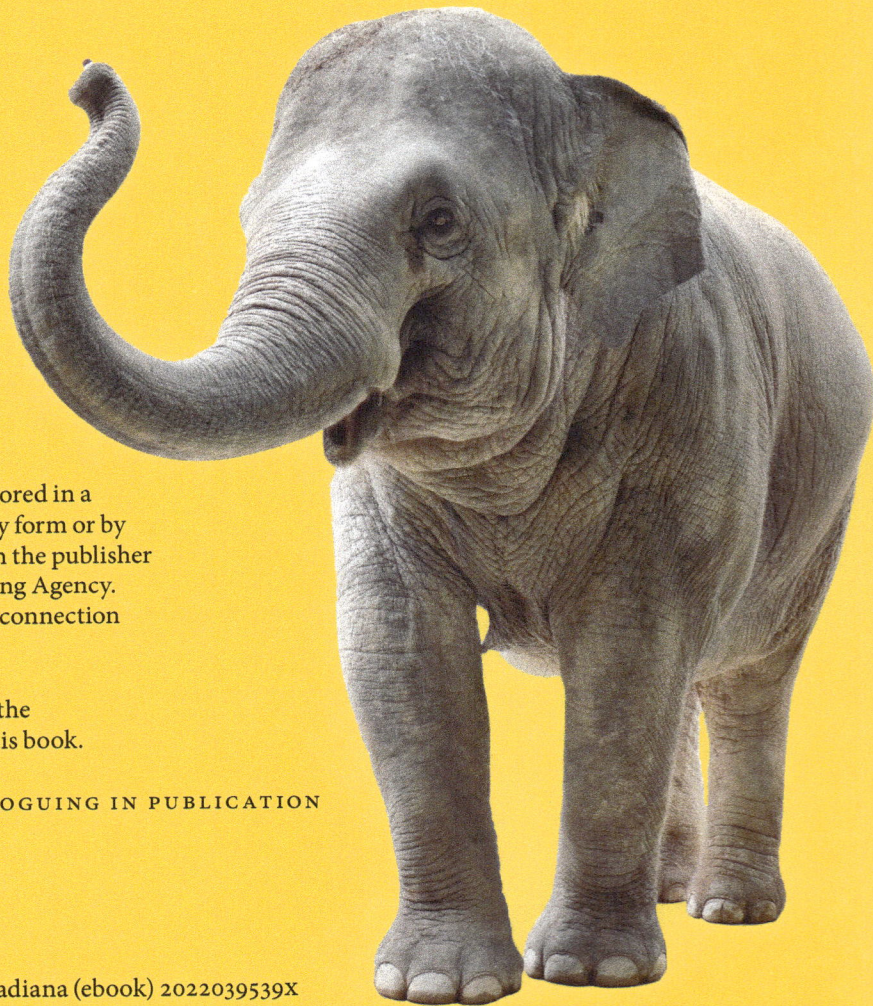

WWW.ENGAGEBOOKS.COM

Elephants and Me
Animals and Me
Harvey, Sarah N., 1950 –
Edited by: A.R. Roumanis
Text © 2022 Engage Books
Design © 2022 Engage Books

Text set in GelPenUpright

FIRST EDITION / FIRST PRINTING

LIBRARY AND ARCHIVES CANADA CATALOGUING IN PUBLICATION

Title: Elephants and me / by Sarah Harvey
Names: Harvey, Sarah N., 1950- author
Description: Series statement: Animals and me

Identifiers: Canadiana (print) 20220395381 | Canadiana (ebook) 2022039539X
ISBN 978-1-77476-680-4 (hardcover)
ISBN 978-1-77476-681-1 (softcover)
ISBN 978-1-77476-682-8 (epub)
ISBN 978-1-77476-683-5 (pdf)

Subjects:
LCSH: Elephants—Juvenile literature.
LCSH: Elephants—Behavior—Juvenile literature.
LCSH: Human behavior—Juvenile literature.

Classification: LCC QL737.P98 H37 2022 | DDC J599.67—DC23

This project has been made possible in part by the Government of Canada.

Canada

What do you know about elephants?

3

Elephants live in groups called herds in Asia and Africa.

Where does your herd live?

Baby elephants are called calves. They can stand up when they are only twenty minutes old.

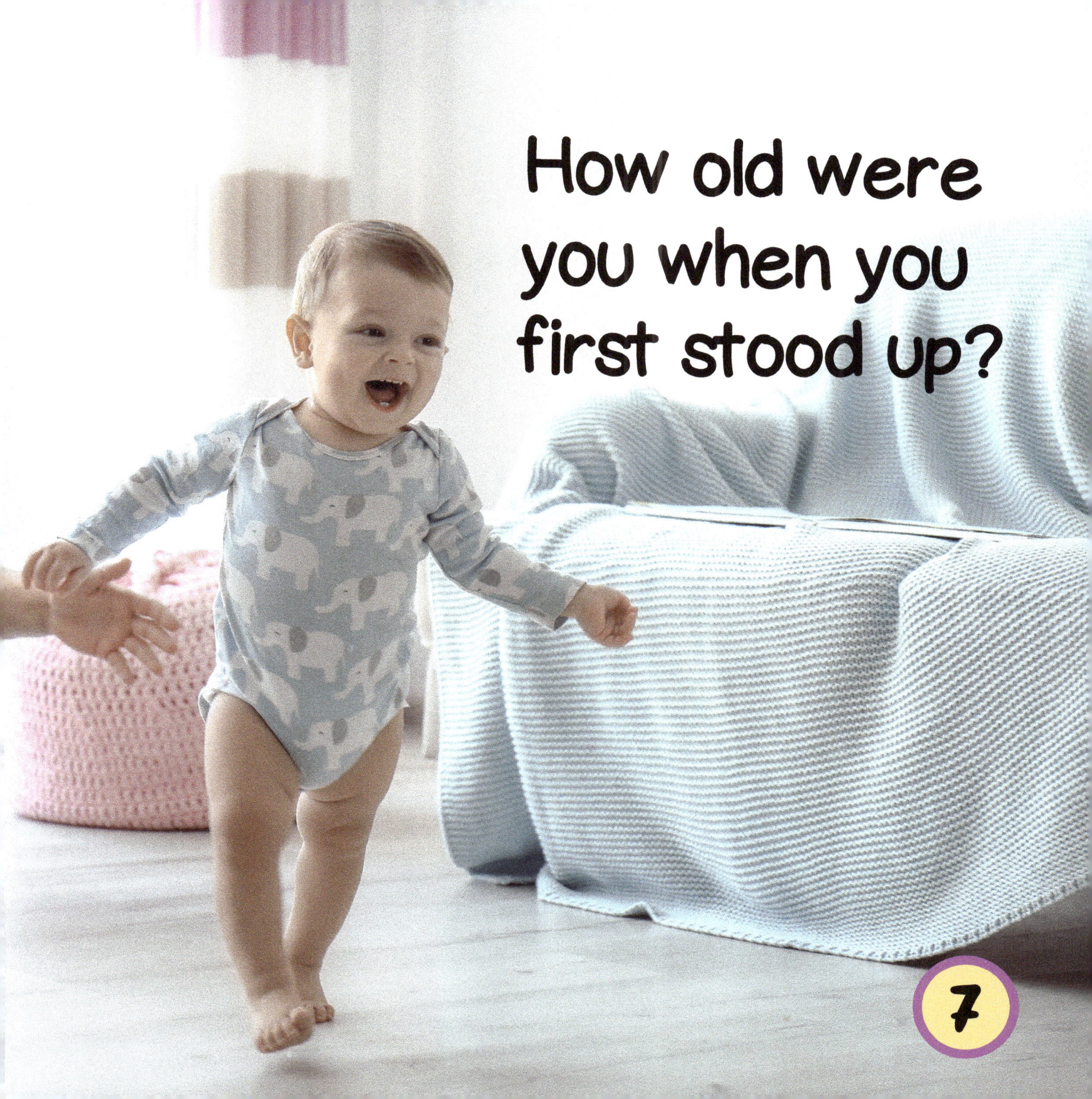

How old were you when you first stood up?

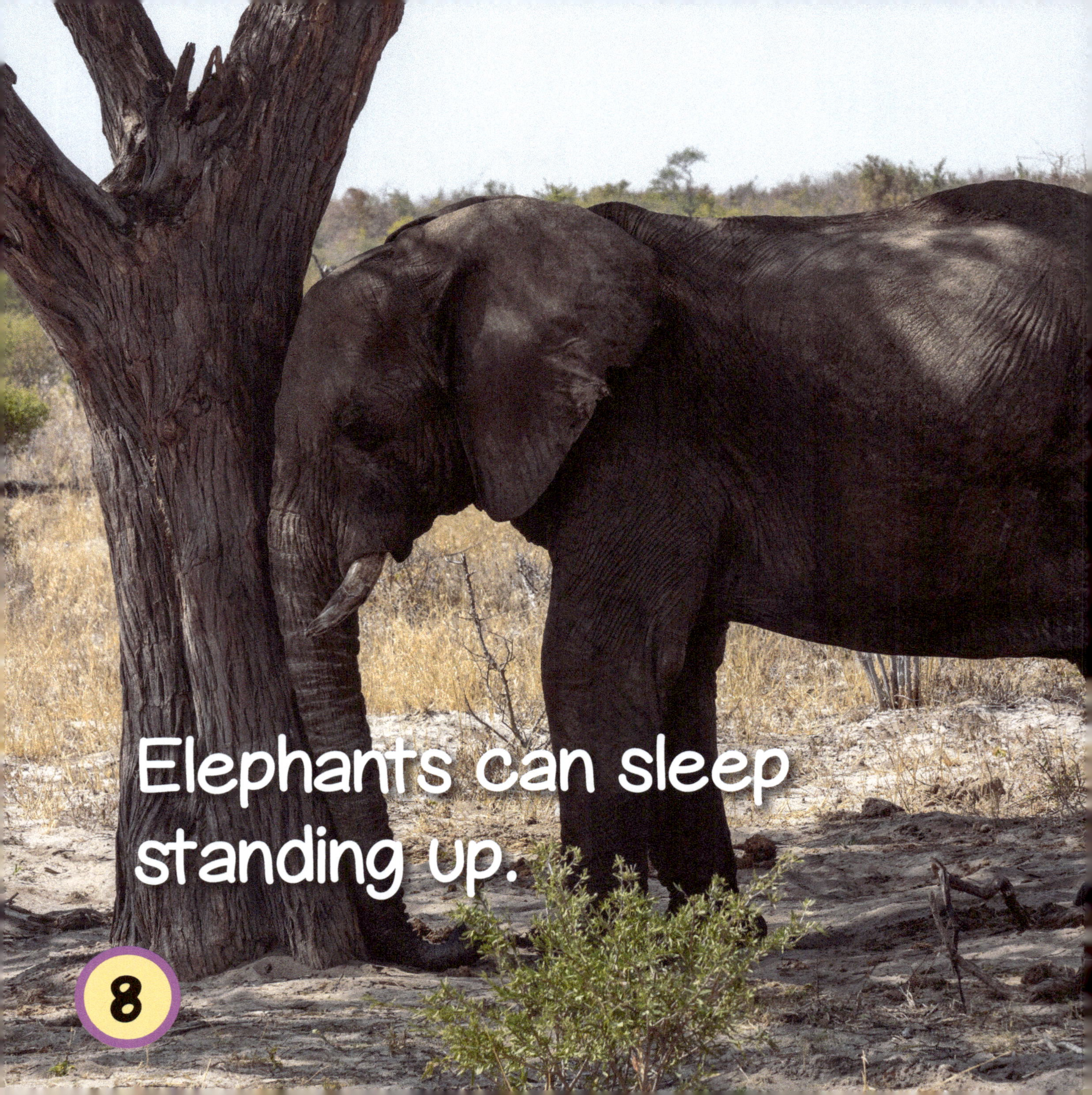

Elephants can sleep standing up.

Where do you
like to sleep?

9

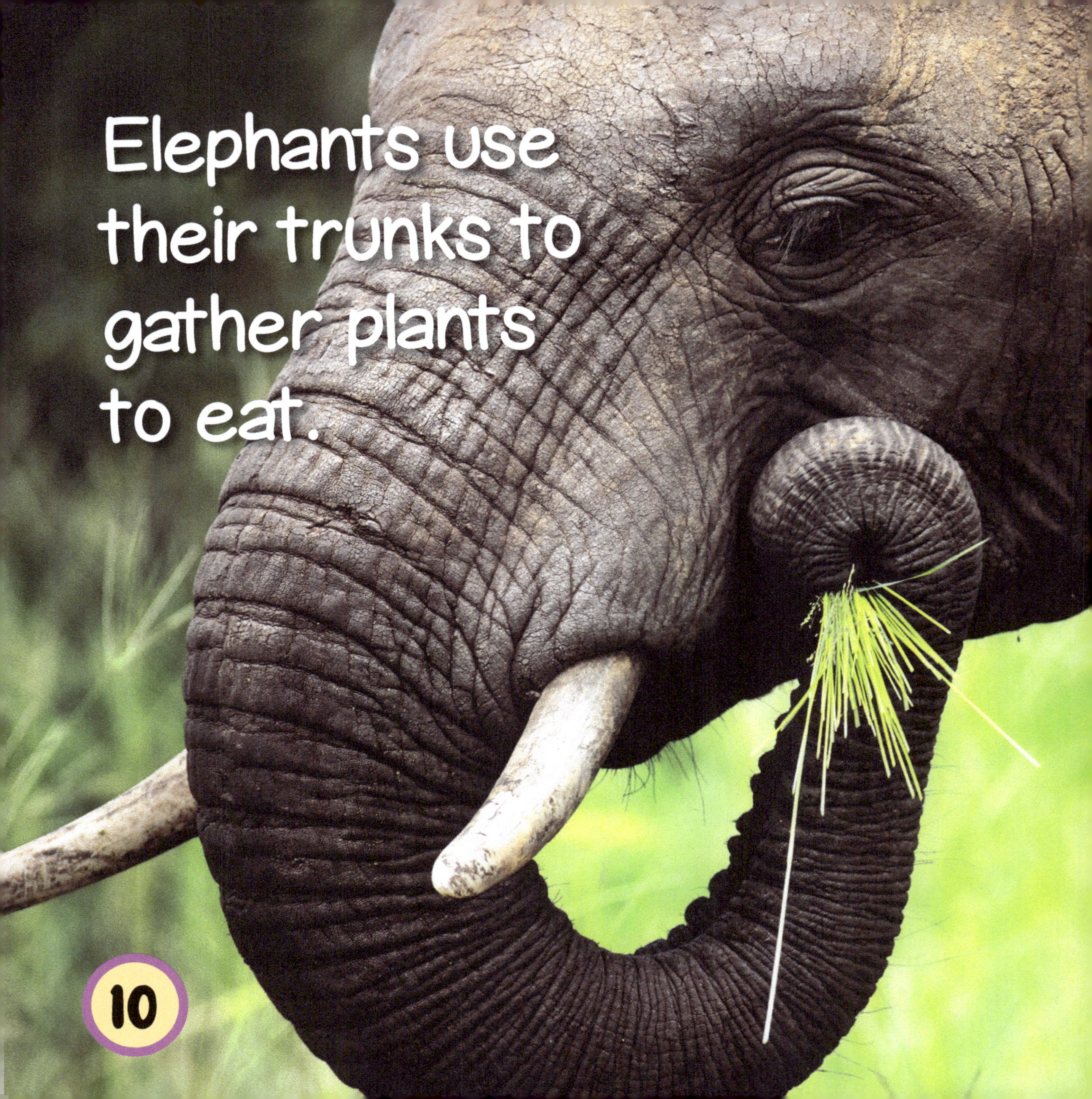
Elephants use their trunks to gather plants to eat.

Do you ever gather your own food?

11

Elephants make friends by smelling and touching each other with their trunks.

How do you make friends?

13

Elephants can live to be very old. They often have lots of children and grandchildren.

Do you know anyone who is very old?

15

Elephants love to be in the water.

Do you like the water too?

17

African elephants use their huge ears as fans to cool down.

18

What do you do to cool down?

Elephants walk very slowly for long distances to find enough food to eat.

Where do you get your food?

Elephants drink over 200 liters of water a day. That's more than a full bathtub of water!

Humans need to drink
lots of water too.
But not that much!

23

Elephants use long sharp teeth called tusks to dig, play, and fight.

Do you use your teeth for anything other than eating?

Elephants can use their trunks like snorkels.

Have you ever been snorkeling?

27

Elephants make their own sunscreen by rolling in the mud.

Don't forget
your sunscreen!

Elephants can grow to be 13 feet tall. But giraffes are way taller.

How tall are you?

www.ingramcontent.com/pod-product-compliance
Lightning Source LLC
Chambersburg PA
CBHW041435040426
42452CB00023B/2981